LEARNING MENTAL ENDURANCE
WITH THE U.S. MARINES

ELITE FORCES SURVIVAL GUIDE SERIES

Elite Survival
Survive in the Desert with the French Foreign Legion
Survive in the Arctic with the Royal Marine Commandos
Survive in the Mountains with the U.S. Rangers and Army
   Mountain Division
Survive in the Jungle with the Special Forces "Green Berets"
Survive in the Wilderness with the Canadian and Australian
   Special Forces
Survive at Sea with the U.S. Navy SEALs
Training to Fight with the Parachute Regiment
The World's Best Soldiers

Elite Operations and Training
Escape and Evasion
Surviving Captivity with the U.S. Air Force
Hostage Rescue with the SAS
How to Pass Elite Forces Selection
Learning Mental Endurance with the U.S. Marines

Special Forces Survival Guidebooks
Survival Equipment
Navigation and Signaling
Surviving Natural Disasters
Using Ropes and Knots
Survival First Aid
Trapping, Fishing, and Plant Food
Urban Survival Techniques

LEARNING MENTAL ENDURANCE
WITH THE U.S. MARINES

CHRIS McNAB

Introduction by Colonel John T. Carney. Jr., USAF–Ret.
President, Special Operations Warrior Foundation

MASON CREST PUBLISHERS

This edition first published in 2003
by Mason Crest Publishers Inc.
370 Reed Road, Broomall, PA, 19008

Library of Congress Cataloging-in-Publication Data available

ISBN 1-59084-013-5

Editorial and design by
Amber Books Ltd.
Bradley's Close
74–77 White Lion Street
London N1 9PF

Project Editor Chris Stone
Designer Simon Thompson
Picture Research Lisa Wren

Printed and bound in Malaysia

10 9 8 7 6 5 4 3 2 1

ACKNOWLEDGMENT

For authenticating this book, the Publishers would like to thank the Public Affairs Offices of the U.S. Special Operations Command, MacDill AFB, FL.; Army Special Operations Command, Fort Bragg, N.C.; Navy Special Warfare Command, Coronado, CA.; and the Air Force Special Operations Command, Hurlbert Field, FL.

IMPORTANT NOTICE

The survival techniques and information described in this publication are for use in dire circumstances where the safety of the individual is at risk. Accordingly, the publisher cannot accept any responsibility for any prosecution or proceedings brought or instituted against any person or body as a result of the uses or misuses of the techniques and information within.

DEDICATION

This book is dedicated to those who perished in the terrorist attacks of September 11, 2001, and to the Special Forces soldiers who continually serve to defend freedom.

Picture Credits
Corbis: 8, 14, 17, 19, 20, 23, 38, 52, 54; **TRH**: 11, 12, 22, 26, 28, 30/31, 33, 34, 36, 40, 42, 46, 50, 55; **US Dept. of Defense**: 24, 43, 44, 48.
Illustrations courtesy of Amber Books and De Agostini UK
Front cover: **TRH** (both)

CONTENTS

INTRODUCTION

Elite forces are the tip of Freedom's spear. These small, special units are universally the first to engage, whether on reconnaissance missions into denied territory for larger, conventional forces or in direct action, surgical operations, preemptive strikes, retaliatory action, and hostage rescues. They lead the way in today's war on terrorism, the war on drugs, the war on transnational unrest, and in humanitarian operations as well as nation building. When large scale warfare erupts, they offer theater commanders a wide variety of unique, unconventional options.

Most such units are regionally oriented, acclimated to the culture and conversant in the languages of the areas where they operate. Since they deploy to those areas regularly, often for combined training exercises with indigenous forces, these elite units also serve as peacetime "global scouts" and "diplomacy multipliers," a beacon of hope for the democratic aspirations of oppressed peoples all over the globe.

Elite forces are truly "quiet professionals": their actions speak louder than words. They are self-motivated, self-confident, versatile, seasoned, mature individuals who rely on teamwork more than daring-do. Unfortunately, theirs is dangerous work. Since "Desert One"—the 1980 attempt to rescue hostages from the U.S. embassy in Tehran, for instance—American special operations forces have suffered casualties in real world operations at close to fifteen times the rate of U.S. conventional forces. By the very nature of the challenges which face special operations forces, training for these elite units has proven even more hazardous.

Thus it's with special pride that I join you in saluting the brave men and women who volunteer to serve in and support these magnificent units and who face such difficult challenges ahead.

Colonel John T. Carney, Jr., USAF–Ret.
President, Special Operations Warrior Foundation

A U.S. Marine applies camouflage cream to his face. His jacket camouflage is the M81 Woodland pattern, introduced in 1980.

THE U.S. MARINE CORPS

The U.S. Marine Corps is one of the world's most effective fighting forces. Equipped with ships, vehicles, and aircraft, the Marines have always shown what it takes to be an elite soldier— their greatest asset being their mental toughness.

The U.S. Marine Corps (**USMC**) was formed in 1775, and it is now the largest elite unit in the world. In battle they have proved their mental toughness time and time again. During World War I, for example, over 13,000 Marines were killed or wounded in the **trenches**. Between the wars, Marines were sent to defend the Pacific islands. Small units were on these islands when Japanese bombers attacked the U.S. Pacific Fleet at **Pearl Harbor** on December 7, 1941.

The subsequent Japanese offensive in the southwest Pacific captured most of New Guinea and part of the Solomon Islands. America had been taken by surprise, and they began a huge fight to push the Japanese back to their homeland. The Marines were asked to help capture the Pacific islands from the Japanese and, in doing so, they fought in some of the bloodiest battles of World War II. Iwo Jima (February to May 1945), for example, was bought with the lives of 6,800 Marines and 900 sailors, and another 20,000 were wounded.

Marine recruits on the obstacle course at Parris Island, South Carolina. The Marine Corps has about 165,000 soldiers on active duty.

Even when the war ended, the Marines did not rest for long. By 1950 they were back in action in the **Korean War,** helping to stop South Korea from being overrun by a communist invasion from North Korea. By now, the Marines' toughness was becoming legendary. In one particular incident, on September 26, 1950, a large force of North Korean tanks and **self-propelled guns** attacked the positions of the 1st Marine Regiment. Despite a ferocious enemy onslaught, the Marines halted the attack, in the process destroying seven tanks and killing over 500 enemy personnel.

Some 12 years later, the Marines were again involved in a war in the Far East: Vietnam. Like Korea, the Marines were used to try and stop communists from North Vietnam taking over South Vietnam. The Marines fought some of the biggest battles of the entire war. One characteristic about the Marines was evident—they would never surrender. In fact, most Marines would be prepared to die rather than lose the fight.

The **Vietnam War** ended in 1975, but the Marines did not have to wait before they were back in action. In October 1983 they were part of a force which went in to rescue over 1,000 U.S. citizens from the small Caribbean island of Grenada. In 1990 the U.S. Marines were part of the Allied forces that liberated the country of Kuwait in the Middle East from the occupation of invading soldiers from Iraq. In September 2001, in response to terrorist attacks on New York and Washington D.C., the Marines were put on the highest level of military alert since the Cuban Missile Crisis of 1962.

Today, the Marine Corps is used all over the world to protect or keep the peace in many countries that are blighted by violence or war.

Not only do the Marines still train to fight hard, but they also perform **humanitarian operations**—distributing food to the starving and protecting people who are afraid of violence. Marines are truly special people. This is why it is so tough to get into the U.S. Marine Corps. One minute they might be in a heavy firefight with the enemy, blazing away with rifles and machine guns. Yet the next minute they might have to be giving first aid to wounded civilians or taking care of children lost in a war zone.

What is obvious is that the Marines must be as tough mentally as they are physically. In this book, you will find out just what sort of mind the U.S. Marine must have if he or she is to maintain over 100 years of proud tradition. By looking at the Marines, we can also learn how to cope with some of the difficult situations that life presents.

Marines on patrol in Grenada. They were sent to this small Caribbean island in 1983 to rescue U.S. citizens.

WHAT YOU NEED TO BE A MARINE

Not everyone is allowed to be a Marine. To join this elite unit, you have to show that you have the right character and intelligence to fight for the reputation of the Marine Corps.

The U.S. Marine is one of the most highly trained soldiers in the world. An average Marine must be courageous, intelligent, able to make decisions quickly, capable of leading men or women into action, good at communicating, writing, and mathematics, and also be able to handle all the weapons at his or her disposal. Because so much is required, trying to get into the Marines is incredibly difficult. We will look at the recruitment process in the next chapter. Here we will see what mental qualities you need to belong to one of the world's best units.

Intelligence

All soldiers must display intelligence, but in elite units the intelligence must be higher than normal. Even in large-scale units such as the U.S. Marines, with 172,000 personnel on active duty, around 90 percent of their entrants are high school graduates. This makes the members of the Marine Corps excellent at working out problems and making decisions on the battlefield. Also,

Since the end of World War II, the Marine Corps has been called on 230 times for combat, peacekeeping, or rescue missions.

military psychologists have studied how intelligence affects the way people fight. They discovered that people who really threw themselves into battle were generally more intelligent than those who did not. They were also better at working out tactics that could win battles. In the elite units like the Marines Corps, an intelligent mind is a must.

Any breach of discipline is dealt with by "Incentive Physical Training." This not only punishes recruits but makes them tougher, too.

Self-control

To be a Marine, you have to be able to discipline yourself. This means doing dangerous, long, boring, or difficult jobs without complaining, and also doing them to the best of your ability. Elite units tend to work in small squads or even as individuals. This means that all soldiers must be able to do their jobs because other people's lives depend on them. A soldier's own self-control could be the only thing that makes a mission a success. Elite forces also spend more time watching and waiting than fighting. They must also be able to deal with the crushing boredom of long, solitary watches while staying alert.

Courage

Throughout their history, the Marines have fought in battles where the odds against them seemed overwhelming. What they need are men and women who

The Dress Blue B uniform is worn only by NCOs and higher ranks.

will not crack under pressure even when things seem desperate. Courage, however, is not something that can be taught. The Marines look for people who show courage in their daily lives, such as standing up for what they feel is right even when everybody else might be against them. Courage is vital because if soldiers do not do their duty in combat, other people's lives may be lost.

Knowledge

One of the duties of a U.S. Marine is to become a "Lifelong Student of the Art of War." The Marines want all their soldiers to be very well informed about military history, tactics, international politics, and foreign cultures, as well as knowing how to fight. That's why all Marines devote a lot of time to reading. They read about how other military leaders have fought wars, and how others have endured in battle. Knowledge of foreign people, places, and languages is also especially valuable. These let soldiers operate more easily on foreign operations in places very different from their homeland.

Resistance to physical pain and discomfort

The Marines' powers of endurance must be formidable by anybody's standards. Marines must be able to withstand running or walking long distances. They must be able to continue fighting even if they have been wounded or have had no sleep for a week. They must be prepared for the capture and violent interrogation that threatens all elite operatives. This is why Marine training is so tough. The drill instructors want to see who can push themselves

Marines are obliged to become "Lifelong Students of the Art of War."
They often read *Warfighting* by General A.M. Gray, written in 1989.

to keep going even when their body feels like it wants to stop. If they cannot keep pushing themselves through the pain of a long-distance run with 80 pounds (36 kg) of **kit** on their backs, then they will probably not have the strength to keep fighting in combat. Only when mental endurance is proven can units have the confidence that their Marines will never give in to adversity.

Team spirit

However much Marines must stand on their own two feet, they must always think of others before themselves. A selfish person will not do well as a Marine. In combat, soldiers must always have confidence in the people next to them. If they do not, then they will not trust each other and will not work together to achieve their mission. If this happens, then the mission will almost certainly fail. True Marines must look after their fellow soldiers as if they were brothers or sisters. The bonds between Marines are incredible. In many instances,

THE INTELLIGENCE CORPS

The old image of the Marines as mindless warriors who thoughtlessly obey orders is totally out of date. Today's Marines must be intelligent and strong-minded, which is the reason why their basic training program is so demanding. They must be capable of thinking for themselves, and working out how to solve problems without asking others.

Recruits who train as a team will lay down their lives for each other in battle. The best size for a combat team is about eight men.

Marines have been known to give their lives while trying to recover the dead bodies of their comrades. This commitment to each other is vital if they are to fight together in battle.

These are just some of the mental qualities demanded of the U.S. Marines, qualities that make them the unique soldiers they are. The will to never give up produces Marines who will stay brave and focused despite the danger all around them.

COPING WITH PRESSURE

Though combat may seem glamorous in the movies, in reality it is a terrifying and sometimes horrifying experience. Some men and women cannot take it, but the Marines try to produce people who can cope with all the pressures of action.

There is a term used to describe the effect that battle can have on your mind—**combat stress**. Combat stress describes what can happen to a human mind when a person spends too long in warfare. Constant explosions and danger, and seeing people being injured or dying, can make even the toughest of soldiers anxious and depressed. Some soldiers are so disturbed by what they see in battle that it affects them for the rest of their lives. The symptoms of combat stress vary a lot between people, but here are some typical feelings.

Aggression and anxiety

Victims feels angry and aggressive. This is not only directed at the enemy, but also at those around them and even at objects. Sometimes it takes only a minor incident such as a loud noise to make these people explode with rage.

For soldiers suffering with anxiety, their lives are troubled by constant worry. It can be so severe that it dramatically affects their

Training takes place at two centers: Parris Island, South Carolina, and San Diego. Each center takes about 23,000 recruits each year.

Marines must show, and are taught, aggression; it prepares them for battle. But recruits must learn to control their aggression levels.

ability to sleep, think, and control their behavior. Symptoms can often include a physical jumpiness.

Apathy and catatonia

Combat-stressed soldiers may show signs of **apathy**. They may mentally withdraw from the outside world and show little interest in the events or situations around them.

Catatonia is an extremely serious medical condition. Victims can physically freeze and be unable to move their limbs, even when other people try to move them with force.

Depression and memory loss

Some veterans become very depressed. This can make soldiers feel very negative about themselves, tired all the time, and worried about what might happen in the future.

In cases where soldiers suffer from memory loss, they may not be able to remember orders even when they were given to them only moments before.

Obsessive activities

Victims repeat actions to no purpose, such as field stripping and assembling their weapons beyond what is normal, or they constantly talk about one subject.

A Marine must keep his M16A2 rifle clean, but the task of cleaning it should not be so frequent that it becomes obsessive.

By preparing Marines for combat through training exercises, it is hoped some of the mental stress associated with battle can be avoided.

Problems with talking

Victims find they are not able to communicate very well, and may even become completely silent.

Trembling

The hands in particular may shake, but this can extend to whole-body trembling in extreme cases.

The U.S. Marines are very aware of these problems and want to protect their soldiers. Their training is designed to prepare soldiers for combat so that they do not become mentally ill. The most vital factor is a process called "**battleproofing**." Battleproofing means that soldiers' training is so realistic that when they go into battle the experience is not so much of a shock. The essence of battleproofing is to make the training scenarios as realistic as possible. This takes away the shock of actual combat.

So how do they do this? A good example is when the Marines are training in urban combat. Fighting in towns and cities is very stressful. Shooting can come from any direction, and soldiers live under this tension for days. During urban warfare training, Marines use a special area at Camp Lejeune, North Carolina, in which a replica city has been built. The Marines are given missions within this city that last for days. During these exercises they have to make lots of decisions under pressure, while machine guns filled with blanks are fired all around them. Sometimes even real bullets are fired just above their heads. Dynamite explosions are set off at a distance that is barely safe. Stun grenades are also used. These impart a huge flash and bang but will not kill or injure. The noise and confusion of these mock battles are almost like the real thing.

Though this is only a training exercise, it must be done with real aggression. It is repeated over and over. It battleproofs the soldiers in several different ways.

Troops can prepare for the stress of warfare through meditation and relaxation.

First, the use of live ammunition helps the soldiers get used to the actual sounds of guns being fired in battle and the noise of bullets whizzing past them.

Second, the Marine gets used to making decisions in noisy and very confusing combat situations. When soldiers finally go into a real battle, they are not as shocked as someone who has not been trained in these true-to-life situations. The U.S. Marines are drilled in these sort of exercises for almost every battlefield situation imaginable. They even conduct huge battles in which aircraft drop large bombs so that the soldiers become accustomed to the huge blasts.

In the first four weeks, the drill instructor will dismiss 15 percent of new recruits. The rest go on to Phase Two—combat training.

The most important thing that helps a Marine to cope with battle is confidence. There are several different types of confidence. For example, Marines are confident that they can make life or death decisions quickly. They are trained so that if the leader of a unit is killed or injured, anyone else can take over as leader. From the moment they arrive at boot camp, Marine recruits are forced to make lots of decisions almost every minute of the day.

Confidence also comes from knowing the soldiers with whom they live and fight. Elite forces train in small, tightly knit groups and come to know and trust one another very well. In combat, this trust makes the group work together as one and become highly motivated. Motivation among soldiers tends to come from the desire not to fail one's comrades and not to let down the regimental name. Consequently, once soldiers have shared months of tough training, they tend to have a high desire to protect and enhance the group. Because of this, soldiers are much less likely to suffer from combat stress because everybody supports everybody else in battle.

MARINES AT ARMS

Marines are given their own M16 rifle when they join. This rifle goes almost everywhere with them. Because they become so familiar with this weapon, they have total confidence that they will know how to use it in battle. Soldiers who are not as well trained will not be able to fire the weapon as accurately in combat.

SURVIVING TRAINING

Before they can become a Marine, the recruits must convince their recruiters that they are suitable. Then they must try to survive the training program, one of the toughest in the world.

All Marine recruits have a long interview before they are allowed to begin training. First, recruits are tested for their level of physical toughness. But they are also assessed for their character and personality. Marine recruiters will probe deeply into the applicants' histories to find moments of courage, determination, or leadership, which may indicate what they will be like as a future Marine. If the individual has struggled through poverty to gain a good education or support a family, this might indicate a strength of mind. If the person was captain of a sports team, it shows that the person can demonstrate leadership. If, however, the person has a criminal record, he or she will be rejected immediately—Marines must respect society and people.

Gradually the recruiter will come to understand the people being interviewed, and form a judgment as to whether they are suitable to be a Marine. Though they may have strong characters, they must also display another mental quality demanded by the Marines—intelligence. All Marines take long intelligence tests. These test skills such as English and mathematics. All Marines must show above-

A Marine has his M16 rifle inspected. The officer is checking that the gun is free from dirt, oiled correctly, and that the barrel is clean.

Clearing land mines is a test of skill. More than 100 million mines remain hidden in old battlefields across the world.

average scores from the tests, making them one of the most intelligent military units in the world.

The Marines also need people in control of their emotions. People who are violent, unpredictable, or unsociable will never make good Marines. However, neither do the Marines want people who do not give enough effort. Elite forces missions tend to require high levels of aggressive commitment. Marines have to have flexible minds that can work out a problem, but they also must pursue their missions with total dedication. This is the quality that we call "mental endurance," and it is this which is tested during training.

For the Marine, there is no such thing as "basic" training. Entering the Marines requires the soldier to undergo incredible physical punishment. For 12 weeks they will be shouted at, forced to run many miles with heavy packs on their backs, deprived of sleep for days at a time, and have to make decisions almost every waking minute. During that time, the candidates are watched to see what their characters are like. The drill instructors are looking for the following qualities.

Tenacity

Can soldiers keep focused on succeeding even when they are physically and mentally at the limits of their endurance? To see

The final few weeks of training are very tough. They include constant physical training, hand-to-hand fighting, and combat exercises.

whether they can, they are put through exhausting marches and physical tasks. If they do these without complaining and with lots of effort, they will earn the drill instructor's approval.

Intelligence

Can soldiers solve problems quickly, even when they are under severe pressure? If they can't, then they won't be any good for the Marines. The ability to think clearly is made more difficult when you are extremely tired or exhausted. This is why the Marine drill instructors push the limits of the soldiers' physical endurance and then see if they are still capable of forming tactical decisions on the battlefield.

Team spirit

Do the candidates help other people succeed and put their own interests second? There is no place in the Marines for those who don't want to cooperate with other people. Team players will also tend to make better tactical thinkers because they ask other people for their opinions rather than assume that they themselves know best.

Self-control

Do the candidates show that they can control their emotions at all times? Marine training often involves two drill instructors shouting different sets of orders at a confused and bewildered recruit. The purpose of this is not to taunt the recruit. Instead, the instructors are watching how he reacts. If he loses his temper and cannot make a decision about what to do, then he will probably not be right for making decisions on the battlefield. However, if he keeps his head, thinks clearly, then makes a decision, this will show the instructors that he has self-control.

Sense of humor

Does the candidate have a sense of humor? This is not just welcome in the Marine Corps, it is essential. Studies conducted during the

Tug-of-war is designed to teach teamwork. However, soldiers who like to work on their own often make good snipers—a solitary job.

The drill instructors watch to see that push-ups are performed properly.
The body is lowered until the upper arms are parallel to the ground.

Korean War found that soldiers with a sense of humor tended to make better fighters. This was because they did not crack under pressure so much, and they improved **morale** in their units.

Training for the Marine Corps is so tough that by the end of the 12 weeks about 20 percent of the recruits will have been rejected. The reasons for this are clear. The Marines are an elite unit. They want only the best because they need to uphold the reputation that they have earned over 200 years of constant striving.

Most Marines will tell you that it is the proudest moment of their lives when they finally go from being recruits to being Marines. The life in the Marine Corps is never easy. Yet wearing the Marine Corps uniform means that they have become a member of the Marine family for the rest of their lives. It also shows that they have the character to succeed in the face of hardship and punishment.

BASIC TRAINING

The U.S. Marines basic training period is designed to be as punishing and demanding as possible. This is because potential recruits may be able to pretend that they are tough for a couple of days, but over a gruelling 12-week period they will not have enough stamina to keep on pretending. Over 12 weeks the Marine officers will be able to assess the recruit's true character.

USING YOUR INTELLIGENCE

In combat, guns and muscle alone will not win the battle. The Marines are trained to constantly outwit their opponents, and use their intelligence to throw the enemy into confusion.

All Marine recruits must have a high score on intelligence tests before they can step into the Marine Corps. It is sometimes puzzling to work out why academic intelligence is so important to soldiers. For some units, it is not as vital. But for elite units like the Marines it is essential. The skills they need break down into four main areas:

• Mathematical intelligence
• Communication skills
• Technical intelligence
• Tactical intelligence

The ability to achieve in each of these areas is an essential requirement in the modern Marine Corps.

Mathematical intelligence

The Marine cannot escape the need to use mathematical skills. Even the act of navigation—a basic requirement for any soldier on land, sea, and air—needs someone to calculate angles, distance, and time.

Signalers radio map coordinates of enemy positions to tanks, artillery, and aircraft, which can then launch attacks.

A Marine with an M47 Dragon anti-tank weapon. He guides the missile to its target by keeping the cross hairs of the sight on the enemy tank.

For the elite soldier, the list of activities that require good mathematical intelligence includes:

- Navigation
- Calculating the right amount of supplies
- Controlling artillery and airstrikes
- Devising secret codes
- Calculating distances
- Estimating enemy troops' strength

From this list, it is clear that mathematics are needed on the battlefield as much as in the barracks. A good illustration of this is the activities of directing **antiaircraft fire** using small arms and artillery control.

Shooting down modern jets using only personal weapons or machine guns is extremely difficult—a modern fighter can be moving at over 900 miles per hour (1,450 km/h) when it flies past. Yet it can be done, and Marines are trained in shooting down aircraft using mathematical calculation. The speed of the aircraft means that they cannot aim straight at it. If they did, by the time the bullets arrived at where the aircraft was, it would already have flown past that point—imagine what would happen if you threw a stone straight at a bird when it was flying by. What is needed is for the aircraft to fly into the stream of bullets coming up from the ground. The Marine needs to calculate a point approximately 650 feet (215 m) from the front of the aircraft. If he or she fires at this imaginary point, then the aircraft will fly directly through their bullets.

This example shows how acts of mathematical intelligence are necessary for fighting. Thus mathematics are thoroughly tested before any individual can become a member of a special forces unit.

Communication skills

Communication skills—the ability to speak and write well—are essential in all walks of life, not just soldiering. Aspiring Marines need to show that they have control over language. On the battlefield, soldiers must be able to tell people clearly and quickly what they want them to do. They must also be able to listen to orders and understand quickly. In combat, any misunderstanding can cost lives. Intelligent use of language for the Marines often means that they acquire foreign languages to help them on international missions. Acquiring another language for military purposes need not be a difficult business. During the Vietnam War, studies conducted in the U.S. Army found that only 450 words were needed to have a basic conversation. In terms of practical languages, English, French, and Spanish are possibly the most useful. This is because these languages are used in more countries around the world than any other languages.

Armored assault vehicles are used for amphibious (water and land) operations. They can carry 25 Marines each, right up onto the beach.

Technical intelligence

Modern Marines are in charge of amazing machines and technology. Even their **M16 rifles** are a complex machine, and soldiers need to understand its engineering to keep it working well. But this is the simplest demand. Marine infantry have an amazing variety of weapons to operate. Each Marine battalion consists of a headquarters company, three rifle companies (each divided into 13-person squads), and a weapons company.

The standard infantry weapons are the M16A2 rifle with a 40-mm grenade launcher attached, and the lightweight 5.56-mm squad automatic weapon (**SAW**) issued to each fire-team. Immediate support is provided by the eight Weapons Company fire-team vehicles armed with half-inch (10-mm) and MK19 40-mm heavy machine guns. Heavy support includes M-60 tanks, 155-mm towed and self-propelled (SP) **howitzers**, eight-inch (200-mm) SP howitzers, 81-mm and 60-mm mortars, and tube-launched, optically-tracked, wire-guided (TOW) anti-tank missile launchers. Air-defense weapons include the effective portable **Stinger** and **Redeye** surface-to-air missile (SAM) systems.

KEEP IT SIMPLE

Tactics should not be too complex. The acronym "KISS" is used in the U.S. forces, standing for "Keep it Simple, Stupid." Marines need to show that they can make clear combat plans that are easy to perform.

Most Marine engineers wear badges depicting castles—the first engineers built forts across the United States during the 1800s.

The technical intelligence needed to operate all these complex weapons is great. It must also be remembered that the Marines operate ships and jets as well. These are the most complex pieces of engineering anywhere in the military.

Tactical intelligence

Tactical intelligence is the ability to work out how to fight most effectively in a particular battle. Marines must consider how to use their strengths against the enemy's weaknesses. They must know how to use their weapons effectively. And they must work out how to move across ground while keeping the danger to themselves and their men to the minimum. One of the key ingredients of tactical intelligence is being able to make decisions. The Marines are taught the "rule of three" when making decisions. For any problem, they come up with three possible solutions (no more, no less). Then they look at what is positive and negative in each, and finally choose one and stick with it. This technique has had great success. By the time the recruits become Marines, they are very comfortable with handling decision-making.

Tactical intelligence requires many different talents—a good eye for detail, a strong memory, the ability to see problems and solutions, a capacity to organize, and the tendency to be able to stick with your decision. The Marine Corps puts intelligence as one of the highest priorities for its soldiers. The fact that the Marines are almost undefeated in battle shows that this emphasis pays off in combat.

Marines receive "Five Paragraph Field Orders," which cover Situation, Mission, Execution, Support, and Command and Signal.

BEING A TEAM PLAYER

All Marines have to work as a team. From the smallest patrol to full divisional operations, everyone has to work together if they are to defeat the enemy.

In combat, a soldier's life often depends on the comrade fighting next to them. That's why the U.S. Marines need people who can help a team of soldiers to success, not just look after themselves. The Marines are capable of huge maneuvers using thousands of people. But regardless of the size of force, it is still governed by what it calls the "rule of three."

In this case, the rule of three means that a Marine's priority is to look after the three individuals or units closest to him or her. Thus, a Marine belongs to a three-person fire team. A Marine sergeant must control a squad of three fire teams. A staff sergeant or lieutenant leads a platoon made up of three squads. Though the number of people involved expands every time they go further up the ladder of rank, the system means that each person has responsibility for a small group of people or unit. The effect of this is that the Marines are very close to one another. This makes Marines more than willing to risk their lives in action for their colleagues. It also helps to make decision-making clear and efficient—a vital factor in the performance of a military unit.

A typical exercise involves carrying someone over the shoulder. This trains Marines to handle a wounded person and also builds trust.

In combat, Marines have to cover other members of their unit. This "Buddy-Buddy" system is also used by the elite British SAS force.

Not all elite units use the same principle of three. However, many other elite units use similar structures. On the smallest scale possible, Britain's Special Air Service (SAS) operate a "Buddy-Buddy" system within all their operations involving two or more people. In arctic warfare or antiguerrilla operations in particular, the soldiers are teamed up in pairs. All soldiers are responsible for protecting their partners and also for stepping in if the partner is killed or injured.

Belonging to an elite

Just the fact that the soldiers are members of an elite force, distinct from the rest of the military world, tends to breed a greater respect for one another. The Marines are dedicated to protect the standards of the regiment and take pride in what they have achieved. In both the British and U.S. Marines (and many other marine forces world-wide), once you have actually been a Marine, you are "a Marine for life." It is not uncommon for Marines who left the service years before, and who find themselves in trouble or going through hard times, to suddenly receive support from their former unit. Marines believe that being a Marine makes you a member of a huge extended family for the rest of your life. Such a sense of belonging is one of the strongest forces for bonding people into a strong team, and this will show itself when entering combat.

Surviving training

During one part of Marine training, the recruits have to run 10 miles (16 km) with an incredibly heavy pack. Part of this run involves a steep hill, known by the recruits as the "grim reaper" because it makes so many people drop from exhaustion. Those that succeed, feel an enormous sense of achievement, which they share with their buddies. These feelings build up trust and intimacy between the Marines throughout the long and difficult training period. Also, the hard training in the Marines eliminates those people who will not help others. The people who are left are those good at teamwork.

Surviving combat

As many Marine veterans have noted, the experience of fighting can change attitudes. The problems that get us down or upset us in civilian life, suddenly seem insignificant. In addition, sharing the experience of fighting can bring together in a bond of friendship people who don't usually like each other . The writer Philip Caputo, a former officer with the U.S. Marines in Vietnam, recounts in his book *A Rumor of War* how two Marines were killed attempting to retrieve the bodies of fallen comrades. They knew that the dead soldiers were beyond help. They knew that going to get the bodies would probably result in their own deaths. Yet they went ahead anyway.

This shows how combat and the Marine family can make the bonds between soldiers extend even to those who are no longer living. Indeed, it is part of the Marine code of honor not to leave the dead behind on the battlefield. Combat brings them even closer together as a team.

A Marine belongs first to the Marine Corps, then to his or her regiment. A Marine regiment consists of about 1,200 men and women.

U.S. MARINES—A TRUE ELITE

Marine training, as we have seen, is ultra tough. Up to 20 percent of people who enter Marine training will not have made the grade at the end of it. But those that survive, form a strong bond. Just the experience of sharing the hopes, pains, and problems of basic training brings soldiers together.

Rituals

A final factor that brings together the Marines as a team are their military rituals and ceremonies. Two of the biggest ceremonies that a Marine experiences take place when a recruit passes training and becomes a full-fledged Marine, and when dealing with the burial of the Marines' dead. The first ceremony, in particular, is one of the most moving of the Marine's life. It is not uncommon for the tough soldiers to cry with the emotion of becoming a member of this elite unit. Once they have been through this ceremony, the sense of pride among all the soldiers is incredible. This pride then makes them work better as a team, because they want to uphold the values of the Marine Corps together.

Many things happen to bring together a group of individual Marines as a team. We have just looked at some of them here. Yet some Marines want to take their role a step further. These men and women want to become leaders of Marines, and that is one of the toughest jobs in the world.

BEING A LEADER

U.S. Marine leaders have to be the best of the best. The soldiers they lead are strong and intelligent, and leaders must inspire them if they are to gain their confidence and lead them into battle.

Character is perhaps the most important element a leader brings to elite units. The reason is to be found in the various mottoes used by elite regiments around the world. Such mottoes include:

SAS	Who Dares Wins
U.S. Army Special Forces	Free from Oppression
Canadian Paratroopers	We Dare
Royal Netherlands Marine Corps	Wherever the World Extends

The motto of the U.S. Marines is "**Semper Fidelis**," a Latin phrase meaning "Always Faithful." The mottoes of the different regiments vary in what they say, but what remains the same is that each holds soldiers to the highest standards of character and demands that they behave with honor and courage.

It is the job of the Marine officers to live up to the values of the unit without exception. They must act as examples to the rest so that others can see how a Marine truly behaves. This is a huge responsibility. Marine recruiting officers have a keen eye on who passes

Officers on parade carry the ceremonial Mameluke sword. It is most often seen during the Marine Corps' birthday on November 10.

Every soldier in the Marine Corps is highly trained with the M16 rifle. It can be fired in either single shots or in three-round bursts.

through their doors to see that they have the right character to stand as an example.

Each Marine leader's character is different—the Marines do not want everybody to be the same. However, there are mental qualities all Marine leaders must have if they are to inspire the people under their command.

Loyalty

Marine leaders must show loyalty to those under their command, the Marine Corps, and the mission they are undertaking. Unless they give all their efforts to their units, and never swerve from that commitment, those under their command will not remain loyal to them. If this happens, the soldiers will not respect the officers, and they will be unhappy about obeying their orders. Yet this does not seem to happen in the Marines. Marine officers are tested in a training program that is even harder than the program the regular Marines endure. At the end, the instructors know exactly who the good people are, and they become Marine officers. That's why one of the greatest motivations behind the soldiers' efforts is to justify their leader's trust. In return, leaders must show that they are good enough to lead some of the best people in the armed forces.

Courage

Marine officers have to possess the courage not only to deal with their own personal danger, but also to demonstrate courage to their whole unit in order to inspire confidence in attack or defense. Courage, however, should not become reckless and overlook the needs of the soldiers. Indeed, Marine officers are taught to put the welfare of those under them above almost everything else. Marine officers should show the courage to keep trying to make the mission succeed while always protecting their soldiers. They should also have the courage to stand up for the values of the Marine even when they meet people who are cynical or mocking.

Integrity

Integrity is slightly different from courage. Integrity for Marine officers means having high personal standards that act as an example to the soldiers under their command. Respect for an officer is something that has to be earned; it is not something that the soldiers

About 250 soldiers apply for each Marine officer training course. Ten percent of these are women. Fifty percent of all applicants will fail.

give automatically. This respect is earned by consistently living up to the values of the unit and regiment. This, in turn, shows that the officer has integrity. The Marine Corps requires officers who have strong morals, and do what is right rather than what is easy. For this reason, the Marines never take former criminals into its ranks—they have shown that they do not have integrity.

Self-denial

Marine officers are there to serve others and not themselves. In combat, and back in the barracks, they must put the welfare of those under their command, the Marine Corps, and their country before that of their own. This means that after a long march officers do not rest like the others. Instead they go around checking that everybody is well, that they have adequate food and water, and that the injured are being treated. In combat, they must be prepared to face every danger and inspire those under them to do the same. They must also take responsibility for all the battlefield decisions and live with the consequences. Only by working for others can Marine officers be true leaders of soldiers.

All the qualities listed must be present in a Marine if he or she is to be a good officer. Yet there are no set of complete rules for how each individual officer should actually behave. The Marine officer in charge of flying a jet will need different skills and talents than a Marine officer in charge of an artillery unit. We have seen that

One Marine ship can launch about 13 Armored Assault Vehicles, which will contain a maximum of 325 Marine soldiers.

Marine officers must have certain qualities to lead. But what does the Marine Corps itself officially say about its officers? What skills and talents do they need if they are to perform well in the hardest place in the world—the battlefield?

In combat, a leader has to cope with enormous levels of distraction. The Marine Corps manual on war—called *Warfighting*—says that the battlefield is dominated by chaos. Situations shift from one second to the next, according to the maneuvers and casualties. Combat officers have to cope not only with the violence of the battle around them, but also try to make tactical decisions in the middle of explosions, surrounded by the dead and injured.

Producing this type of leader is never easy. The training must be hard, realistic, and stressful in order to test who will crack under the pressure and who will be able to fight on. In the U.S. Marines, the officer graduate is meant to emerge at the end of training with a clear set of skills and aptitudes. Officers have to be adept at several roles.

Leaders/Commanders

They must show that they can actually lead in action, inspiring others to follow them. They need the courage to see a difficult mission completed to the best of their ability.

Decision makers and communicators

Marine officers must be able to make good decisions very quickly. If they can think more quickly than the enemy, they can win the battle.

Officers also need to be able to communicate orders. Their orders must be clear and straightforward, so being able to communicate efficiently is a vital skill for Marine officers.

Warfighters/Executors

Marine officers are combat officers. They must show that they know how to fight wars, and that they can design battle-winning tactics.

Lifelong students of the "Art of War"

Because they are combat officers, Marines should always study the ways of war to keep learning. This means talking to veterans, reading military history, and studying tactics.

If they can perform these five roles, then Marine officers will become good leaders of soldiers. As with everything in the Marines, the recruits have to work extremely hard to achieve their goals. Being a good Marine officer takes years of commitment and experience to achieve. But for those who rise to the challenge, and for all the soldiers of the Marine Corps, nothing beats the feeling of knowing they are among the best.

QUALITIES OF THE MARINE OFFICER

Apart from loyalty, courage, integrity, and self-discipline, there are a whole range of other qualities that the Marine officer must have. These qualities include self-motivation, enthusiasm, a sense of humor, and an eye for detail.

GLOSSARY

Antiaircraft fire Shooting designed to bring down enemy aircraft.

Apathy The feeling that nothing really matters and that there is no point in trying to do anything.

Battleproofing The process of putting soldiers through realistic training so that they do not mentally crack in combat.

Catatonia A mental problem in which the victim goes completely stiff and is unable to move.

Combat stress The psychological problems that can occur in soldiers who have experienced combat.

Gulf War A war in the Middle East that occurred after Iraq invaded the country of Kuwait.

Howitzers Large artillery weapons that fire very powerful shells.

Humanitarian operations Nonaggressive missions that help civilian people in trouble.

Kit The Marine's equipment and clothing.

Korean War A war between North and South Korea, fought between 1950 and 1953, which involved the U.S. and other nations.

M16 rifles Standard rifles of today's U.S. forces.

Morale In military terms, the confidence and discipline present in a unit of soldiers.

Pearl Harbor The harbor of the U.S. fleet, which was bombed by the Japanese on December 7, 1941.

Redeye An antiaircraft missile system used by the U.S. Marines.

SAW Squad Automatic Weapon—the light machine gun used by U.S. military forces.

Self-propelled guns Artillery weapons that are mounted on tracks like a tank.

Semper Fidelis A Latin phrase meaning "Always Faithful," the motto of the U.S. Marines.

Speed march A march done at a faster pace than normal.

Stinger An antiaircraft missile system used by the U.S. Marines.

Tenacity The quality of determination and never giving up, no matter how tough things become.

Trenches Much of the conflict of World War I was fought by soldiers dug into deep ditches for months on end.

USMC The abbreviation of United States Marine Corps.

Vietnam War A war in the Far East, in which the U.S. fought between 1965 and 1973.

Warfighting The name of one of the Marines' most influential books on how to fight wars.

CHRONOLOGY

November 10, 1775	Marines Corps formed by Act of Congress.
1801–1805	Marines battle with pirates throughout the Mediterranean and across the north coast of Africa.
1812–1814	Marines fight against the British Navy during wars over shipping and territory.
1846–1848	Marines fight in the Mexican-American War.
1861–1865	Marines fight in the American Civil War.
1917–1918	U.S. enters into World War I. Marines lose 13,000 men in the trenches of the Western Front.
August 7, 1942	The U.S. Marines make their first big amphibious operation of the war at Guadalcanal in the Solomon Islands. The battle that follows lasts six months.
November 20, 1943	5,500 Marines take the Japanese-held island of Tarawa, but suffer over 1,000 dead.
June 15, 1944	The battle of Saipan begins. The Marines capture the island but lose 3,426 soldiers, though 29,000 Japanese soldiers are killed.
February 19, 1945	The battle for the island of Iwo Jima, the Marines' bloodiest battle in its history, begins. The Marines suffer 21,000 casualties, but capture the island.
April 1, 1945	The battle for Okinawa begins, and the Marines fight alongside the 10th U.S. Army.
1950–1952	The Marines fight in the Korean War. Great actions include the amphibious landings at Inchon and the battle with the Chinese army at the Chosin Reservoir.

1962	Marine units start to become involved in a growing war in Vietnam.
March 1965	Large-scale units of Marines land in Vietnam, the first dedicated combat troops of the Vietnam War. Marines were involved in the war until 1975.
January–March 1968	A garrison of Marines endure a 77-day siege at Khe Sanh, Vietnam, when the communist North Vietnamese Army launched a major invasion of South Vietnam.
October 1983	Marines form a significant part of a U.S. mission to rescue U.S. citizens from the Caribbean island of Grenada.
1990–1991	The Gulf War. U.S. Marines make up part of the massive Allied force that liberates Kuwait from the soldiers of Iraq.
1992–Present	Marines conduct peacekeeping actions in Bosnia-Herzegovina, former Yugoslavia.
1992	USMC troops are deployed in Somalia, Africa, on peacekeeping operations.
1994	Marines form part of U.S. invasion of Haiti in effort to restore democracy there.
1998	Marines help Kenyan citizens and four South American countries recover from natural disasters.
1999–2001	Marines are used to keep the peace in Kosovo in Operation Allied Force.
September 11, 2001	In response to terrorist attacks, the U.S. military, including the Marine Corps, are put on the highest level of military alert since the Cuban Missile Crisis.

RECRUITMENT INFORMATION

The entry requirements for the U.S. Marines are:

- You must be between 18 and 29 years old, though 17-year-old applicants will be considered with parental consent.
- You must be a high school graduate.
- You must be of "high moral character." (For instance, you must not have a criminal record or a history of taking drugs.)

If you are accepted for training, you go on to 12 weeks of recruit training. This is a tough training program and up to 20 percent of recruits don't pass. If you do, then you are a member of the Marine Corps and you will go on to four weeks of Marine combat training (MCT).

To find out more, check out these web sites:
http://www.marines.com
http://www.usmc.mil/
http://www.media.euro.apple.com
http://www.marzone.com
http://www.hqmc.usmc.mil
http://www.inc.com/users/wma1.html
http://mcia-inc.org
http://www.ibiblio.org/hyperwar/USMC/USMC-I.html

You can also talk to Marine recruiters by dailing:
1–800–MARINES.

FURTHER READING

Alexander, Joseph H. *The Battle History of the U.S. Marines: A Fellowship of Valor.* New York: Harper Perennial Library, 1999.

Halberstadt, Hans. *U.S. Marine Corps (The Power Series).* Osceola, Wis.: Motorbooks International, 1993.

Leckie, Robert. *Strong Men Armed: The United States Marines Against Japan.* New York: Da Capo Press, 1997.

Simmons, Edwin. *United States Marines: A History.* Annapolis, Ma.: Naval Institute Press, 1998.

Voeller, Edward. *US Marine Corps Special Forces: Recon Marines.* Minnetonka, Minn.: Capstone Press, 1999.

ABOUT THE AUTHOR

Dr. Chris McNab has written and edited numerous books on military history and elite forces survival. His publications to date includes *German Paratroopers of World War II, The Illustrated History of the Vietnam War, First Aid Survival Manual,* and *Special Forces Endurance Techniques,* as well as many articles and features in other works. Forthcoming publications include books on the SAS, while Chris's wider research interests lie in literature and ancient history. Chris lives in South Wales, U.K.

INDEX

References in italics refer to illustrations